Published by
Lion Publishing plc
Sandy Lane West, Oxford, England
ISBN 0 7459 2911 7
Lion Publishing
850 North Grove Avenue, Elgin, Illinois 60120, USA
ISBN 0 7459 2911 7
Albatross Books Pty Ltd
PO Box 320, Sutherland, NSW 2232, Australia
ISBN 0 7324 0825 3

First edition 1994
10 9 8 7 6 5 4 3 2 1

Acknowledgments
All photographs by Willie Rauch; except Oxford Scientific Films: A
Hive of Activity, Audrey Palmer: Unsung Flowers, Silver Drops of
Dew, A World of Wonder; Peter Stiles: The Hope of Spring, A
Moment's Glory, Artistry beyond Compare; ZEFA: Into the Garden,
Flowers of Paradise.

A catalogue record for this book is available
from the British Library

Printed and bound in Malaysia

Inspired by Flowers

BEVERLEY PARKIN

A LION BOOK

Introduction

When I was nine years old, I had to learn the poem 'Daffodils', by William Wordsworth. I fear it was learned by rote with very little understanding of its meaning. However, on recitation of the piece I was given a book of poetry. It took pride of place on my book shelves with its vivid yellow cover, although it was many years before I actually read it! Then I was fascinated by the words, amazed at the insights of the poets, and enjoyed the ability of these men and women to conjure up, in my mind, word pictures that transcended the narrowness of the world in which I lived at that time.

Books are friends, many turned to over and over again — how I loved *The Secret Garden*! From hospital beds when young, to putting up one's feet when getting older, the written word can be a delight when the subject matter is dear to the heart.

For centuries, flowers have inspired poets to their great works — either in praise for the flowers themselves or for their resemblance to the human form and its foibles.

Some of the pieces in this book may be as new to you as they are to me, but the old faithfuls are there — still causing us to stop and savour the thoughts and capture the scene in our mind's eye.

I always feel that poems should be read aloud, the words chewed over — a veritable feast of good things — to see and experience the dew, the joy of a shady spot, the cottage garden, the breeze of spring amongst the daffodils, the heavy sweet air perfumed by the honeysuckle — such delights have inspired writers to their greatest works. Words can transport us to different cultures, unusual perspectives, up into space and down into the delicate detail of a flower. God's infinite variety knows no end to all these wonders.

No words of mine can possibly match those that follow, but let me encourage you to close your eyes and imagine the pictures that the authors are describing.

God has given us so much to enjoy, either in difficult times when the going is tough, or when there is time to relax and ponder. His care for us is shown in the world of nature. A rose will never seem the same again! Even the humble daisy declares 'in sweetest smelling bloom ... your Maker and my God.'

BEVERLEY PARKIN

Into the Garden

I t was the sweetest, most mysterious-looking place anyone could imagine. The high walls which shut it in were covered with the leafless stems of climbing roses, which were so thick that they were matted together... All the ground was covered with grass of a wintry brown, and out of it grew clumps of bushes which were surely rose-bushes if they were alive. There were numbers of standard roses which had so spread their branches that they were like little trees. There were other trees in the garden, and one of the things which made the place look strangest and loveliest was that climbing roses had run all over them and swung down long tendrils which made light swaying curtains, and here and there they had caught at each other or at a far-reaching branch and had crept from one tree to another and made lovely bridges of themselves. There were neither leaves nor roses on them now, and Mary did not know whether they were dead or alive, but their thin grey or brown branches and sprays looked like a sort of hazy mantle spreading over everything, walls, and trees and even brown grass, where they had fallen from their fastenings and run along the ground. It was this hazy tangle from tree to tree which made it all look so mysterious. Mary had thought it must be different from other gardens which had not been left all by themselves so long; and indeed it was different from any other place she had ever seen in her life.

'How still it is!' she whispered. 'How still.'

FROM *THE SECRET GARDEN*, FRANCES HODGSON BURNETT

Wayside Flowers

Dear common flower, that grow'st beside the way,
Fringing the dusty road with harmless gold,
   First pledge of blithesome May,
Which children pluck, and full of pride, uphold.
How like a prodigal doth nature seem,
When thou, for all thy gold so common art!
   Thou teachest me to deem
More sacredly of every human heart,
Since each reflects in joy its scanty gleam
   Of heaven.

JAMES RUSSELL LOWELL

The rose that with your earthly eyes you see,
   Has flowered in God from all eternity.

ANGELUS SILESIUS

A Precious Place

A garden is a lovesome thing, God wot!
   Rose plot,
   Fringed pool,
Fern'd grot —
   The veriest school
   Of peace; and yet the fool
Contends that God is not —
Not God! in gardens! when the eve is cool?
   Nay; but I have a sign;
   Tis very sure God walks in mine.

'MY GARDEN', T.E. BROWN

My sweetheart, my bride, is a secret garden,
   a walled garden, a private spring;
   there the plants flourish.
They grow like an orchard of pomegranate-trees
   and bear the finest fruits . . .
Fountains water the garden,
   streams of flowing water,
   brooks gushing down from the Lebanon Mountains.

FROM THE SONG OF SONGS

The Carol of the Flowers

Lord Jesus hath a garden, full of flowers gay,
Where you and I can gather nosegays all the day:

    There angels sing in jubilant ring,
  With dulcimers and lutes,
    And harps, and cymbals, trumpets, pipes,
  And gentle, soothing flutes.

There bloometh white the lily, flower of Purity;
The fragrant violet hides there, sweet Humility:

The rose's name is Patience, pruned to greater might;
The marigold's, Obedience, plentiful and bright:

And Hope and Faith are there; but of these three the best
Is Love, whose crown-imperial spreads o'er all the rest:

And one thing fairest is in all that lovely maze,
The gardener, Jesus Christ, whom all the flowers praise:

O Jesus, all my good and bliss! Ah me!
Thy garden make my heart, which ready is for thee!

'THE GARDEN OF JESUS', DUTCH CAROL

The Hope of Spring

If I might see another Spring
I'd not plant summer flowers and wait:
I'd have my crocuses at once,
My leafless pink mezereoris,
My chill-veined snowdrops, choicer yet
My white or azure violet,
Leaf-nested primrose; anything
To blow at once not late.

FROM 'ANOTHER SPRING', CHRISTINA ROSSETTI

For snowdrops are the harbinger of spring,
A sort of link between dumb life and light,
Freshness preserved amid all withering,
Bloom in the midst of grey and frostly blight,
Pale stars that gladden Nature's dreary night.

CAROLINE NORTON

Care for all Creation

N ot even King Solomon with all his wealth had clothes as beautiful as one of these flowers. It is God who clothes the wild grass — grass that is here today and gone tomorrow, burnt up in the oven. Won't he be all the more sure to clothe you? How little faith you have!

JESUS' WORDS IN THE GOSPEL OF MATTHEW

A child said, What is the grass? fetching it to me with full
*   hands;*
How could I answer the child? I do not know what it is any
*   more than he.*

I guess it must be the flag of my disposition, out of hopeful
*   green stuff woven.*

Or I guess it is the handkerchief of the Lord,
A scented gift and remembrancer designedly dropt,
Bearing the owner's name someway in the corners, that we
*   may see and remark, Whose?*

FROM 'SONG OF MYSELF', WALT WHITMAN

The Character of Flowers

F lowers are the sweetest things God ever made and forgot to put a soul into. Flowers have an expression of countenance as much as men or animals. Some seem to smile, some have a bad expression, some are pensive and diffident, others again are plain, honest and upright like the broad-faced sunflower and the hollyhock.

HENRY WARD BEECHER

While men cultivate flowers below, God cultivates flowers above; He takes charge of the pastures of heaven. Is not the rainbow a faint vision of God's face?

H.D. THOREAU

The Mystery of Flowers

Flower in the crannied wall,
I pluck you out of the crannies; —
Hold you here, root and all, in my hand,
Little flower — but if I could understand
What you are, root and all, and all in all,
I should know what God and man is.

'FLOWER IN THE CRANNIED WALL', ALFRED LORD TENNYSON

To see a world in a grain of sand
And a heaven in a wild flower
Hold infinity in the palm of your hand
And eternity in an hour.

WILLIAM BLAKE

Artistry beyond Compare

Bowing adorers of the gale,
Ye cowslips delicately pale,
   Upraise your loaded stems,
Unfold your cups in splendour; speak!
Who deck'd you with that ruddy streak,
   And gilt your golden gems?

Violets, sweet tenants of the shade,
In purple's richest pride array'd,
   Your errand here fulfil!
Go, bid the artist's simple stain
Your lustre imitate, in vain,
   And match your Maker's skill.

Daisies, ye flowers of lowly birth,
Embroid'rers of the carpet earth,
   That stud the velvet sod;
Open to spring's refreshing air,
In sweetest smiling bloom declare
   Your Maker and my God.

'SPRING FLOWERS', JOHN CLARE

A Garden for all Seasons

G od Almighty first planted a garden. And, indeed, it is the purest of human pleasures. It is the greatest refreshment to the spirits of man, without which buildings and palaces are but gross handyworks: and a man shall ever see, that when ages grow to civility and elegancy, men come to build stately, sooner than to garden finely; as if gardening were the greater perfection.

I do hold it, in the royal ordering of gardens, there ought to be gardens for all the months in the year: in which, severally, things of beauty, may be then in season.

FRANCIS BACON

Nothing is so beautiful as Spring
When weeds, in wheels, shoot long and lovely and lush.

FROM 'SPRING', GERALD MANLEY HOPKINS

A Hive of Activity

I know of nothing so pleasant as to sit in the shade of that dark bower, with the eye resting on that bright piece of colour, lighted so gloriously by the evening sun, now catching a glimpse of the little birds as they fly rapidly in and out of their nests — for there are always two or more birds' nests in the thick tapestry of cherry trees, honeysuckle and china roses which cover our walls — now tracing the gay symbols of the common butterflies as they sport around the dahlias; now watching that rare moth, which the country people, fertile in pretty names, call the bee-bird; that bird-like insect which flutters in the hottest days over the sweetest flowers, inserting its long proboscis into the small tube of the jessamine, and hovering over the scarlet blossoms of the geranium, whose bright colour seems reflected on its own feathery breast.

FROM *OUR VILLAGE*, MARY RUSSELL MITFORD

Unsung Flowers

A s many herbs and flowers with their fragrant sweet smells do comfort and as it were revive the spirits and perfume a whole house; even so such men who live virtuously, labouring to do good, and to profit the Church of God and the commonwealth do as it were send forth a pleasing savour of sweet instructions, not only to that time wherein they live and are fresh, but being dry, withered and dead, cease not in all after ages to do as much or more.

Many herbs and flowers that have small beauty or savour to recommend them, have much more good and virtue: So many men of excellent rare parts and good qualities do lie unknown and not respected, until time and use of them do set forth their properties.

JOHN PARKINSON

Flowers of Paradise

Once in a dream I saw the flowers
That bud and bloom in Paradise;
More fair they are than waking eyes
Have seen in all this world of ours.
And faint the perfume-bearing rose,
And faint the lily on its stem,
And faint the perfect violet
Compared with them.

FROM 'PARADISE: IN A DREAM', CHRISTINA ROSSETTI

I will give water to the thirsty land
and make streams flow on the dry ground;
I will pour out my spirit on your children
and my blessing on your descendants.
They will thrive like well-watered grass,
like willows by streams of running water.

FROM THE BOOK OF ISAIAH

Each Season's Beauty

Were all the year one constant sunshine, we
  Should have no flowers,
All would be drought and leanness; not a tree
  Would make us bowers;
Beauty consists in colours; and that's best
Which is not fixed, but flies and flowers.

HENRY VAUGHAN

Though nothing can bring back the hour
Of splendour in the grass, of glory in the flower;
We will grieve not, rather find
Strength in what remains behind.

WILLIAM WORDSWORTH

Silver Drops of Dew

The dewdrops on every blade of grass are so much like silver drops that I am obliged to stoop down as I walk to see if they are pearls — and those sprinkled on the ivy-woven beds of primroses underneath the hazels, whitethorns and maples are so like gold beads that I stooped down to feel if they were hard, but they melted from my finger. And where the dew lies on the primrose, the violet and whitethorn leaves, they are emerald and beryl, yet nothing more than the dews of the morning on the budding leaves, nay, the road grasses are covered with gold and silver beads and the further we go the brighter they seem to shine, like solid gold and silver. It is nothing more than the sun's light and shade upon them in the dewy morning; every thorn-point and every bramble-spear has its trembling ornament; till the wind gets a little brisker, and then all is shaken off, and all the shining jewellery passes away into a common spring morning, full of budding leaves, primroses, violets, vernal speedwell, bluebell and orchids and commonplace objects.

JOHN CLARE

A Moment's Glory

Fair daffodils, we weep to see
You haste away so soon;
As yet the early-rising sun
Has not attained his moon
      Stay, stay
Until the hasting day
      Has run
But to the even-song;
And having prayed together, we
Will go with you along.

We have short time to stay, as you.

ROBERT HERRICK

Do not fear to hope . . .
Each time we smell the autumn's dying scent,
We know that primrose time will come again.

SAMUEL TAYLOR COLERIDGE

In Unexpected Places

I saw a delicate flower had grown up two feet high, between the horses' path and the wheel-track. An inch more to the right or left had sealed its fate, or an inch higher; and yet it lived to flourish as much as if it had a thousand acres of untrodden space around it, and never knew the danger it ocurred. It did not borrow trouble, nor invite an evil fate by apprehending it.

HENRY DAVID THOREAU

Bright flower! whose home is everywhere,
Bold in maternal Nature's care,
And all the long year through the heir
Of joy and sorrow;
Methinks that there abides in thee
Some concord with humanity,
Given to no other flower I see
The forest thorough!

WILLIAM WORDSWORTH

Shout for Joy

T here was music. Big poppies and peonies blew on pods of sweet peas with such vigour that their faces were red. The bluebells tingled. It was a funny orchestra both to look at and to listen to. At last came all the other flowers dancing; violets, daisies and lilies of the valley; as they finished their dance, they kissed each other. It was lovely to see.

HANS CHRISTIAN ANDERSON

You will leave Babylon with joy;
you will be led out of the city in peace.
The mountains and hills will burst into singing,
and the trees will shout for joy.
Cypress-trees will grow where now there are briars;
myrtle-trees will come up in place of thorns.

FROM THE BOOK OF ISAIAH

A World of Wonder

There is a world of wonder in this rose;
God made it, and his whole creation grows
To a point of perfect beauty
In this garden plot. He knows
The poet's thrill
On this June morning, as he sees
His will
To beauty taking form, his word
Made flesh, and dwelling among men.
All mysteries
In this one flower meet
And intertwine,
The universal is concrete
The human and divine,
In one unique and perfect thing, are fused
Into a unity of Love . . .
The tears
Of Christ are in it
And his blood had dyed it red,
I could not see it but for him
Because he led
Me to the love of God,
From which all beauty springs.
I and my rose
Are one.

'THE ROSE', G.A. STUDDERT KENNEDY